1006076226

The ABC's of

of

A survival guide for today's office worker

GAYE MERCER

Outskirts Press, Inc.
Denver, Colorado

The opinions expressed in this manuscript are solely the opinions of the author and do not represent the opinions or thoughts of the publisher. The author has represented and warranted full ownership and/or legal right to publish all the materials in this book.

The ABC's of How to BE
A survival guide for todays office worker
All Rights Reserved.
Copyright © 2009 Gaye Mercer
V2.0

This book may not be reproduced, transmitted, or stored in whole or in part by any means, including graphic, electronic, or mechanical without the express written consent of the publisher except in the case of brief quotations embodied in critical articles and reviews.

Outskirts Press, Inc.
http://www.outskirtspress.com

ISBN: 978-1-4327-3786-3

Library of Congress Control Number: 2008942412

Outskirts Press and the "OP" logo are trademarks belonging to Outskirts Press, Inc.

PRINTED IN THE UNITED STATES OF AMERICA

Have you recently applied for or
been offered
a cushy office job?

Perhaps you already work in such a job
but find yourself
unable to
move up the ladder.

If so, then this book is for you.
It will help you get
acclimated
to the world of
politics,
double-speak
and mumbo-jumbo.
It will undoubtedly prepare you
to be
the best
YOU CAN BE.

CONTENTS

A
Be ACCEPTING - 3
Be ACCOUNTABLE - 4
Be ARTICULATE - 5
Be ATTENTIVE - 6
Be AWARE - 7

B
Be BUSY - 11
Be BRAVE - 12

C
Be COGNIZANT - 15
Be COLLABORATIVE - 16
Be CREATIVE - 17

D
Be DEDICATED - 21
Be DUTIFUL - 22

E
Be ENTHUSIASTIC - 25

F
Be FLEXIBLE - 29

G
Be GAY - 33
Be a GOOD SPORT - 34

H
Be HELPFUL - 37
Be HONEST - 38
Be HUMBLE - 39

I
Be INCLUSIVE - 43
Be INNOVATIVE - 44
Be INSPIRING - 45

J
Be like JELLO - 49

K
Be KEEN - 53

L
Be a LEADER - 57
Be LOW-KEY - 58

M
Be a MENTOR - 61

N
Be NICE - 65

O
Be ORGANIZED - 69
Be OPEN - 70

P
Be POSITIVE - 73
Be PROACTIVE - 74
Be PRODUCTIVE - 75
Be PROFESSIONAL - 76
Be PROMPT - 77
Be PRUDENT - 78

Q
Be QUIET - 81

R
Be RESPECTFUL - 85

S
Be SENSATIVE - 89
Be of SERVICE - 90

Be SKILLFUL - 91
Be SMART - 92
Be SUPPORTIVE - 93

T

Be a TEAM-PLAYER - 97
Be TRUTHFUL - 98

U

Be UNDERSTANDING -101

V

Be a VISIONARY - 105

W

Be WILLING - 109

X, Y & Z

Be X, Y and Z - 111

BE ACCEPTING

You will soon learn
not everyone cares
about being a good employee.
Some people are loafers, some are mean,
some are thieves and some are
patently ignorant.
Be patient; these creeps
will eventually
go away (hopefully).
In the mean time
relax
and turn a blind eye.
Above all, don't mention their
misconduct to your boss.
Tattle-tellers
don't usually make it very far.

BE ACCOUNTABLE

It's important
to understand exactly
what is expected
of you.
Talk to your boss
if you have questions or concerns.
The last thing you need
is to be responsible
for someone else's work
or mistakes.
You also need to understand
that even you
will make mistakes
now and then.
But don't worry, no one is perfect.
Just smile and say
"I'm sorry."

BE ARTICULATE

Learn how to
insert as many words
as possible into a sentence
and as many sentences
into a paragraph.
It's also a good idea to repeat the
information in your document at least
three times
and more if possible.
That way
you'll be prepared
when you need to create a form
for your customers
or write a report
for
upper management.

BE ATTENTIVE

Don't think
beyond your scope of work.
If you do
you might see something
that
doesn't make sense.

Besides, you don't want
to understand
someone else's job
because you'll end up having
to do it
when they go
on vacation
or
get fired.

BE AWARE

There will be days when
on-the-job stress
will be more than you can handle; so
much so that you might be tempted to
partake in an alcoholic drink
during lunch.
This is okay as long as it's on your time
and you don't get inebriated.
More important is
where you go and with whom.
You can't be seen drinking alcohol
unless you're part of
upper management.

If that's the case, then
no worries…drinking is required.

B

BE BUSY

Today's cubicle offices make it virtually impossible to do anything without being seen.
Sometimes you just can't win, no matter what you do. If you are seen talking to a coworker in the hallway or outside smoking on the sidewalk you are perceived to be wasting time.
If you need to talk to someone use your cell phone at your desk or tell them to meet you in the supply room.
If you smoke go out to your car.
Above all, carry a file or briefcase wherever you go so you look like you're on a mission.
The key is to keep moving and keep out of sight.

BE BRAVE

Don't be afraid
when you witness your boss
behaving in incomprehensible ways.
You must never call that behavior out.
If you do
you run the risk of being
tagged
and
being tagged
is worse
than being fired.
So when those instances pop up
be brave and look the other way.
Someday
you might want
their job.

c

BE COGNIZANT

It's important
to always do your best
and set a good example for others.
Executive management loves to see this
because
if you look good they look good.
A wee note of caution though, especially
if you happen to be an over-achiever.
Those above you,
even if they say otherwise,
do not like to be shown up. You can't
appear to be brighter than they are.
The key is to remember
to slip up now and then
so they can come to your rescue and
you can remind them why they get paid
the big bucks.

BE COLLABORATIVE

You will find that
most work processes
involve other people, work units, offices
and sometimes
completely different businesses.
You'll hear that it's
important to work with them
as business changes and develops
because you're all part of
"the system."

Don't be surprised, though, when "small"
changes are kept quiet….
no sense in getting everyone involved.
Besides, everyone will figure it out
eventually.

BE CREATIVE

Today's world
is becoming more and more dependent
upon visual effects and
abbreviated language.
It's becoming harder and harder
to communicate without using
pictures, bullets and icons.
So whenever you have
meetings with your boss it's always
a good idea
to bring your white board and box of dry-
erase marker pens
so that you can draw pictures
as you speak.
Believe me, what you draw
will leave more of an impression
than anything
you'll have to say.

D

BE DEDICATED

The only golden rule
that will never be mentioned
but should always be
foremost on your list of no-no's
is saying (to anyone)
"I don't have enough to do."
Don't even try to disguise it like
"Is there anything else I can help with?"
or
"Wow, I'm all caught up."

Failure to follow this rule will
undoubtedly land you
a pink slip
or at best
a job in Timbuktu
swatting flies.
That's a fact, Jack.

BE DUTIFUL

Don't be surprised
if you see poor performers
receive a
thank-you card from your CEO.

What you have to remember is
CEO's can't be perceived
as being un-fair.
They believe it takes everyone to get the
job done.
Besides, such acts of kindness
promote inclusion.

So be mindful of your own duties and
above all
be thankful
you got a card
too.

E

BE ENTHUSIASTIC

You'll find that maintaining
passion
for your job can be tough.
When you find yourself in that situation
try to remember your first day on the job.
What was the motivating factor
for getting out of bed
and going to work that day?
Was it because you thought you could
make a difference? If it was, well….
wake up, slap your face and forget that.
The reality is
you are expendable
like everyone else you work with.
The best thing you can do for yourself is
focus on the end result,
i.e. the paycheck.
The sooner you do this the better.

F

BE
FLEXIBLE

As you will soon learn
business changes quite frequently.
It is wise to be flexible
and go with the flow.
When you are asked to
change something don't concern yourself
– you'll just get frustrated.
In fact, never question
management's decisions.
If you see a problem, don't worry.
It's not your responsibility
to tell them – it's more important
to save face.
Besides, they didn't ask for your input
did they?
It's just best to let them find out
and then come to you
for help.

G

BE GAY

It's important
to maintain a sense of joviality
and humor
in the workplace.
Goodness knows how difficult it is
to go to work every day of the week
and be happy about it.

Some folks create a gay atmosphere by
telling jokes
or coming up with
witty remarks.
And this is okay – everyone needs a
laugh now and then. However you must
make sure your boss isn't within
earshot....
especially if they aren't the jovial type.
Need I say more?

BE
A GOOD SPORT

If you are a quick learner chances are
you will be asked
to pick up the slack
for some of your coworkers.
It's amazing how many people just can't
seem to get their work completed
on time
or accurately.
Don't worry; it happens to the best of us.
Just think of how you're setting
a good example
by helping
your
less fortunate peers.
Without a doubt your
good deeds will not go unrecognized and
before long you'll be asked to do
even more.

H

BE HELPFUL

Always smile and say
"okay"
whenever anyone asks you
to do something.
If you don't want to do it, don't do it.
If they ask you about it
all you need to say is:
"Oh, is that what you wanted? I must've
misunderstood…when did you
need that by?"
or
"Maybe we should review that again."
or
"Sorry, I have to make a call –
can we get together
later on this?"

BE HONEST

We all know
honesty
is always the best policy.
In fact I don't know of an organization
that doesn't value honesty.
The key
is to understand exactly what
honesty means.
What is generally means is
unless you have something nice to say,
don't say anything.
And if you have
something to say that is not so nice,
wait until you find a way to say it nicely.
And by all means
keep smiling because
nobody likes to see a frown.

BE HUMBLE

Every year you should expect
to be appraised for your performance. It's
one way to know that your boss
is paying attention
and is appreciative of your hard work.
You will most likely be graded
accordingly as to how you:
a.   smiled at all the unit meetings
b.   didn't complain about any of your coworkers
c.   and showed up for work at least eighty percent of the time
As for your output,
well that really doesn't matter…the
important thing is
you tried.

I

BE INCLUSIVE

It's important
to establish and foster
good working relationships.
In fact, the buddy system
works really well if you work in one of
those offices with micro-cubes.
I suggest you buddy up with one of
your peers.
The first thing you should do is swap
your computer login passwords.
That way you'll always be able to log
in to each other's PC if one of you
happens to be running late or needs a
couple of hours for shoe shopping.
It's amazing how long a person can be
stuck at the copy machine or in the
bath room.

BE INNOVATIVE

If you see a work process
that could be done more efficiently
don't say anything before asking
your supervisor what
they
think.
Don't worry if you don't get credit
for the great idea
because
it will probably cost someone their job
or cause problems
in another part of the office.
You don't want to be seen as a
goody-two-shoes.
Besides, everyone's happy
with the way things are.
Why fix what's not broken?

BE INSPIRING

Never say
what's really on your mind.
When someone says
"How are you?"
Believe me
they don't want to know.
Keep on hand a list of platitudes
like these:

a. I'm just peachy
b. We're really busy
c. Things are looking up
d. Life is a box of chocolates
e. The team is coming together
f. Today is just lovely, isn't it?

J

BE LIKE JELL-O

Undoubtedly you will hear through the
grapevine things about you.
Chances are they won't be
good things simply because people don't
care to talk about the good;
they only get off on telling the bad.
And the truth, well.... what is the truth?
So be prepared to let this stuff
bounce right off.
Grow a thick skin and don't take
anything anyone says seriously.
If you don't, you will find your ego
joining in the mud-slinging.
You'll get a temporary feel-good fix that
will only serve to validate
the bad things
that weren't true in the first place.

BE KEEN

There will come a time, to be sure, when you will encounter a boss who just doesn't like you.
Be alert to the subtle signs of which there can be many. Here are a few:
  a. passive-aggressive comments about your skills and attributes
  b. withholding key information
  c. frequent last-minute cancellations of your one-on-one meetings

If you encounter any one of these it's important that you don't call attention to the disgusting behavior. You have two choices- wait for your pink slip or find another job. It's that simple.

L

BE A LEADER

There are all kinds of books out there that describe what a leader is and how to be an effective one.
It's a good idea to read up on as many as possible; memorize the author's names and all the current buzz words.
They'll come in handy when you're interviewing or talking to executives.
Who knows….you might learn something new.
The truth of the matter is if you want to be an effective leader all you have to do is learn how to follow whoever's in charge because <u>*you never are*</u>.
Nothing too complicated there.

BE LOW-KEY

It's amazing how fast new information
grows wings in the workplace –
especially when it's
supposed to be a secret.
People just can't help themselves; they
have to communicate to each other.
It's important to stay out of the fray but
also stay informed. So when someone
comes to you with a juicy tidbit
be prepared with an exit plan like:
"Oh my, I think I hear my phone!" or
"Gee whiz, I have to go to the
bathroom!"
or "Do you know what time it is?"
Above all, make sure you aren't seen
talking to any known trouble-makers; we
all know how powerful
perceptions are.

BE A MENTOR

It's a good idea to be open to share your
knowledge and experience.
This works
as long as you don't get too
in-depth.
It's always a smart idea to keep some
things to your self.
You should never want those
you're mentoring
to get ahead
too fast.
Remember, too much information
makes people ask questions
and questions
always cause confusion
and
confusion causes problems.

BE
NICE

You will find
a lot of people you work with
don't exactly act their age.
That's because these folks never left the
schoolyard. When they get mad at you
instead of talking to your face they set in
motion what's called a circle jerk. They
run to their boss who in turn runs to your
boss, who, more times than not, gets the
story all wrong and you get the lashing.
So play it safe by pretending you're in
the second grade and
you'll get along just fine.
Remember the playground rules:
no hitting, shoving, scratching or name
calling; no crowding or spitting at the
water fountain; and by all means
keep your tongue in your mouth.

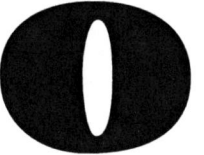

BE ORGANIZED

It's a good idea to keep
a diary
of daily events.
This takes time but you'll find
the information will come in handy.
Remember
if it's not written down
it didn't happen
or
it didn't get said.

It's amazing how some people
never remember
what happened yesterday,
let alone, last month.
Take my advice and write it down.
You won't regret it.

BE OPEN

Be careful if your CEO
makes it a habit to tout his/her
open-door policy,
especially when they act like they're
your best friend.
I know the idea of being offered private
time with the big cheese might seem
exciting but you must realize their sole
intent is to find out what makes you tick
and use it against you.
They will give you the false impression
that you are more important than you are
so you will feel free to divulge things
you know or think you know about
other people.
It might be okay to open the window
but never open the door.
Trust me.

P

BE POSITIVE

It is important to present a demeanor of
industrious optimism.
We must always
put our best foot forward
and bear any disagreeable situation
with a smile.
If you find yourself becoming
tense or irritable while participating in a
meeting or discussion,
take a deep breath
and take your mind to another place.
Staring out the window or a hole
in the wall helps.

Don't worry if you miss anything;
you can always request
another meeting.

BE PROACTIVE

Whenever you come across
a situation that reflects
negatively on your boss and
you know how to fix it,
don't.
This is critical, especially if your boss is
known to bring in experts for everything.
It's better to casually mention the fix
at a time when your boss is really busy.
Believe me,
when the s--- hits the fan,
you won't have any problem
getting your idea implemented
and you'll probably
be nominated
for
employee of the year.

BE PRODUCTIVE

Forget
about working fast
or diligent.
The key is to spread your work out
at
a
steady
slow
pace.
If you need
to triple-check your output
in order to make this work,
that's okay.
In fact
you'll probably get
recognized
for your
attention to detail.

BE PROFESSIONAL

Dress appropriately
depending on your level of authority.
If you are first line staff,
anything goes – just make sure your
midsection is covered (well, mostly) and
your t-shirt logo doesn't express
recognizable profanity or lewdness.
Second-line staff, the same applies,
however I don't recommend shorts cut
above the knees or flip-flops.
If you're mid-management, khaki slacks
and polo shirts work well.
Upper management, without exception,
must be clad in
polished wool suits and ties,
panty hose, pumps, polyester and pearls.
The p-p-p-plainer you are the better.

BE PROMPT

Don't come to work
any earlier
than ten minutes
before your shift begins.

Arriving any earlier
means
you have one or a combination
of the following problems:

- d. you're mentally ill
- e. you're a brown-noser
- f. you're broke and living out of your car (i.e., addicted to alcohol, drugs, gambling)

BE PRUDENT

Don't worry
about how many copies you need to
make or how many times it took you to
get something copied right.
Paper is cheap –
besides you're not paying for it.

And those neat gel pens…no one will
ever guess who took a whole box of them
home
the other night.

It sure pays to stay late
once
in a while.

9

BE QUIET

One of the hardest things to overcome is
the temptation to talk about others
in your workplace.
This is not about being nice, believe me.
It's all about protecting you and
your future.
If you *have* to say something negative
then remember to always counter-
balance it with a positive, like:
"I'm so glad I don't work for him any
more….but don't get me wrong,
I still like the guy."
or
"She's a total nut case…but
she's a lot of fun at parties!"
The fact of the matter is, no one really
cares what you think….they only care
about ratting on you.

R

BE RESPECTFUL

Smile
at everyone
including
that
weirdo
with the bad teeth
and
nauseating body odor.

If you don't
you aren't being the team player
who respects
a diverse workforce.
Besides, he'll probably be your boss
sooner
than you think.

BE SENSATIVE

You may be tempted
to approach a fellow worker
in another unit
in an attempt to understand
why they did what they did
before handing the work off to you….
after all, you're all part of the
same team, right?
Wrong.
First of all, you should never
assume something is actually wrong,
worse is actually acting on that suspicion.
Be sensitive.
Call and make an appointment
to meet in a neutral space
to discuss the issue.
That way feelings won't get hurt.

BE
OF SERVICE

If you get
a disgruntled customer
on the phone
put them on hold
for at least a minute.
When you get back to them
tell them
you cannot locate their records
and
you'll have to call them back tomorrow.
Then throw away their number.

No sense in talking to anyone
when they're upset.
Let them call back when
they
feel better.

BE SKILLFUL

The workplace
is full
of differing ideas, thoughts
and opinions.
It can be difficult to talk about
controversial issues
among such diversified groups.
If you must enter into a conversation
be sure that you speak
to all sides of the issue and
never let on to anyone
what your opinion actually is.
This is what is referred to as
speaking out of both sides of your mouth
– an art worth practicing
every day,
religiously.

BE SMART

The world is full of people from different walks of life and we must respect them for that. Differences don't only mean the obvious things like religion, customs, and language.
It also means differences in regards to learning.
You will find that people fit into a handful of learning styles. Some learn by hearing; some learn by hearing and seeing; some learn by hearing, seeing, and doing; and some learn by hearing, seeing, doing and saying.
The smarter ones simply learn to say they have a different learning style.
Not a complicated strategy but it always works.

BE SUPPORTIVE

Invent a story
around a family member
that lives in another city or state;
someone who is sick and lives alone that
you'll need to periodically go
and take care of.
That way
you'll always have
a legitimate reason
to take leave.
At the very least
you'll have a reason to miss
boring all-day meetings
and
those phony office-wide
"let's get to know each other"
events.

T

BE
A TEAM PLAYER

Always volunteer
for committees and work groups.
It will make a positive impression
on your boss.
You need to remember though when you
attend committee meetings
that you don't say too much
and above all
don't volunteer for anything.
That's because there's always those
executive wanna-be's
who will take over and do it all anyway.
It's best to sit still and smile. If you're
asked to complete a task respond with
"Well….I don't know…."
Before you know it, a wanna-be will be
jumping at the opportunity
to help you out and do it all for you.

BE TRUTHFUL

Keep your mouth shut when you attend
team-building seminars
where you're asked to bear your soul –
especially when in the company of
executive management – unless you
happen to be one of those on the very
bottom of the totem pole.
This is because executives (the highly
educated) believe folks at the very
bottom (the uneducated)
possess a child-like quality therefore they
will see things for what they are
and speak the truth.
Just remember…if you happen to be one
of those at the bottom of the pole,
you are also at the bottom of the hill.
And you know what happens
when the s--- starts rolling.

BE UNDERSTANDING

If you happen to have one of those
coveted government jobs you will most likely find
the pay is not the greatest
and there are no fringe benefits.

As for pay raises
you might get one
or you might not,
it all depends.
And as far as promises go,
well they can be broken.
Keep your chin up;
John Q. Public
is proud
of your sacrifice.
You can take that to the bank.

BE
A VISIONARY

We all have had,
at some time or another,
ideas that come to us from
out of the blue.
It's important to capture those ideas.
It's also important to keep those
wonderful ideas in a safe place.
I say this because there will be people
that just don't understand. In fact, it's
probably just as well that you don't
mention your ideas unless you do so in
private. Let your boss decide
if the idea is any good.
You'll want to be saved from any
embarrassment; besides, you should let
them mull it over
and revise it if necessary.
A total win-win situation.

BE WILLING

One of the most important things
you can do for yourself
is to ignore the fact that
you are human.
It's imperative
that you keep your emotions in check
at all times, regardless.
I say this because there are a lot of
people who just don't like to deal with
others' unhappiness or for that matter,
their happiness.
Learn to put on your office face
before you walk in the door.
Smile but not too broadly,
people will read something into it.
And by all means make sure
no one ever sees
you cry.

X, Y & Z

BE
X, Y & Z

It can be said that much if not all of our world is based on perception and the office workplace is no exception.
It's hard to navigate let alone stay afloat in such changing waters. But you must understand the minute you enter the workforce, regardless if public or private, you become a politician –
like it or not.
And the political world is one where perception rules. It's a world where you are asked to be X, Y or Z on any given day. It's up to you to figure out exactly what X, Y and Z are because today they might be *this* and tomorrow *that.*
The key is to be a chameleon; blend in with your surroundings and by all means never lose or give away your oars.

THE END

Printed in the United States
136754LV00002B/129/P